T0170112

IN THE
NATIONAL INTEREST

General Sir John Monash once exhorted a graduating class to 'equip yourself for life, not solely for your own benefit but for the benefit of the whole community'. At the university established in his name, we repeat this statement to our own graduating classes, to acknowledge how important it is that common or public good flows from education.

Universities spread and build on the knowledge they acquire through scholarship in many ways, well beyond the transmission of this learning through education. It is a necessary part of a university's role to debate its findings, not only with other researchers and scholars, but also with the broader community in which it resides.

Publishing for the benefit of society is an important part of a university's commitment to free intellectual inquiry. A university provides civil space for such inquiry by its scholars, as well as for investigations by public intellectuals and expert practitioners.

This series, In the National Interest, embodies Monash University's mission to extend knowledge and encourage informed debate about matters of great significance to Australia's future.

Professor Margaret Gardner AC
President and Vice-Chancellor,
Monash University

KATE FITZ-GIBBON

OUR NATIONAL SHAME: VIOLENCE AGAINST WOMEN

MONASH
UNIVERSITY
PUBLISHING

Monash University Publishing
Matheson Library Annexe
40 Exhibition Walk
Monash University
Clayton, Victoria 3800, Australia
https://publishing.monash.edu

Monash University Publishing brings to the world publications which advance the best traditions of humane and enlightened thought.

ISBN: 9781922464675 (paperback)
ISBN: 9781922464682 (ebook)

Series: In the National Interest
Editor: Louise Adler
Project manager & copyeditor: Paul Smitz
Designer: Peter Long
Typesetter: Cannon Typesetting
Proofreader: Gillian Armitage
Printed in Australia by Ligare Book Printers

A catalogue record for this book is available from the National Library of Australia.

To my trio: Matilda, William and Edward.
You are my driving motivation for
demanding change.

OUR NATIONAL SHAME: VIOLENCE AGAINST WOMEN

Within the whirlwind of a global pandemic, a second crisis is tearing at Australia: violence against women. For me, this grim national emergency has long permeated our community, and it was further emphasised by events that surfaced at the start of this year.

In February 2021, former Australian Parliament staffer Brittany Higgins alleged that she had been raped by a male colleague in a minister's office at Parliament House in Canberra in March 2019. The allegation made national headlines and prompted a next-day apology from Prime Minister Scott Morrison, who described it as a 'wake-up call' for parliament.[1] Less than a fortnight later, a historical rape allegation emerged against a then-anonymous

Cabinet minister—who was later revealed to be the then Commonwealth attorney-general, Christian Porter—sparking a frenzy of speculation in the media and further calls for national leadership on violence against women. These events were instrumental in reigniting a movement to demand gender equality and justice, and to put an end to violence against women in Australia.

The allegations coincided with International Women's Day on 8 March. The timing was perfect: as the media daily reported on acts of sexual violence and gender discrimination in the federal parliament, women used IWD to take to stages, lecterns and virtual events across Australia and decry the current state of affairs in our highest places of power. They also demanded action, pondering whether this was the Me Too moment for Australian politics.

A week later, on Monday 15 March, a huge number of women—and some men—marched in forty cities and towns across the country. March 4 Justice saw over 110 000 Australians come together to demand change.[2] I marched in Melbourne alongside government and university colleagues. Standing in the

Treasury Gardens, I listened to incredible women share their own experiences of violence and call for greatly improved responses. It felt like this could be *the* moment. Collectively, women were angry, but there was also a feeling of power and hope for change. But while I shared that hope in the moment, my optimism was shattered only hours later when I read the comments made by the Prime Minister, who had crudely boasted:

> It is good and right, Mr Speaker, that so many are able to gather here in this way, whether in our capital or elsewhere, and to do so peacefully to express their concerns and their very genuine and real frustrations ... Not far from here, such marches, even now, are being met with bullets, but not here in this country. This is a triumph of democracy when we see these things take place.[3]

Was this really what our Prime Minister had to say in response to this historic call from his constituents? Leadership matters—a lack of meaningful and effective leadership at the highest level of government on violence against women is the biggest barrier to achieving genuine reform.

The Prime Minister's reaction—which is the type of dismissive reaction that has been offered by many in positions of power and influence—to allegations of violence against women in every corner of the country, from Parliament House to Australian households, tells me that this is both a crisis and a source of national shame. Again and again, the reality of violence in the everyday lives of Australian women is dismissed. All too often, the seriously damaging actions of the men who perpetrate this violence are explained away by everyone from politicians to CEOs. Some institutions in Australia turn a blind eye to violence against women, be they political, legal or corporate. Simultaneously, the service sector is buckling under the enormous number of incidents that require attention. It is shameful that a country with tremendous resources and a system of government that is capable of coordinating a national response that prioritises women's safety, has failed to do so.

We are in a stalemate in which the prevalence rates of violence against women are stubbornly persistent.

While we have had moments of widespread despair, collective calls to action, and some sustained periods of media attention on the issue, our national response quite simply has not been good enough.

It is not good enough, for instance, that it has now been seven years since eleven-year-old Luke Batty was killed by his father, Greg Anderson, and we are yet to see any meaningful institutional, structural and attitudinal change at the national level—something that Luke's mother, 2015 Australian of the Year Rosie Batty, has campaigned so hard for.

Luke's story is both heartbreaking and illustrative. In February 2014, in an act of premeditated violence, Luke was beaten and stabbed to death by his father at cricket practice in the outer-Melbourne suburb of Tyabb. The coroner's inquest found there had been a series of 'missed opportunities' to intervene in the case, and that numerous organisations had been ineffectual in only partially identifying the risk Luke faced.[4]

Incidents like this are devastatingly unremarkable: every fortnight in Australia, a child is killed by their parent(s).[5] In any given year, this equates on average to the killing of twenty-seven Australian children. What proved remarkable in Luke's case was Rosie Batty's courage in the immediate aftermath of her son's death. The very next day, she spoke to the media in front of her house, and for me, her words cut through the problem of family violence in an intensely powerful way:

> I want to tell people that family violence happens to [anybody], no matter how nice your house is, no matter how intelligent you are. When you're involved with family violence, friends, family judge you, the woman—the decisions you should make, the decisions you don't make. You're the victim, but you become the person that people condemn … What I want people to take from this is that it isn't simple. People judge you, people tell you what you should do. You do the best you can.[6]

Re-reading Rosie's words now, I am still struck by their power. At the time, the public reaction to them seemed to indicate that Rosie's message was being heard, that Australia might finally and fully *get it.* In 2015 she was named Australian of the Year, and over the next twelve months she spoke at 250 public events and attended countless meetings with politicians. She was ever-present in the media and, as a result, the issue of family violence was ever-present in the national conversation in a way that I'd never seen before. The outrage provoked by Luke's death also has been credited with propelling family violence onto the political agenda—in Victoria, it was a significant impetus behind the establishment of Australia's first (and the only) Royal Commission into Family Violence.[7]

Seven years on, though, I feel deflated. While Rosie Batty paved a significant path forward, there has nonetheless been both a lack of progress and the continuity of men's violence in Australia. Indeed, women and children continue to be killed at the same rate as in 2014—and these cases are just the tip of the iceberg, a devastating level of destruction in the lives of women and children experiencing domestic and family violence.

Violence against women is an issue that often seems to be as invisible as it is pernicious. Over a five-day period in late October 2018, six Australian women were killed by violent men.[8] Surely this warranted a significant response. Yet these incidents elicited little outcry and even less political acknowledgement or demands for action. Imagine the political reaction and the media attention if six Australians were all killed by the same unnatural cause in any other week.

Journalist Jane Gilmour described the relative silence at the time like this: 'Our compassion is fatigued by the daily drain of women being beaten, raped, assaulted, ignored, dismissed, blamed, ridiculed, murdered. How exhausted we all are by the violence women live and die with'.[9] Six days after Gilmour wrote about this 'compassion fatigue', the death toll had climbed to eight women killed by men's violence in Australia in ten days.

Are we to maintain, as Gilmore does, that the rate of violence against women means Australians simply don't have the emotional capacity to give sustained attention to this issue? I cannot agree with this fatalistic assessment. To acknowledge it is to concede that I live in a country that doesn't value women's lives.

One thing that is abundantly clear to me is that sustained national leadership on violence against women is needed to point (and fund) the way forward, but at present we have a leadership vacuum. The responses of the federal leaders who spoke in the wake of recent allegations of sexual violence in Parliament House were found wanting. As for those federal leaders who remained silent—and there are notable ones in the political ranks—their lack of courage and conviction on this issue also has been noted.

I can only hope that 2021 is *the* catalyst year for the transformative change we so desperately need to address violence against women in Australia.

BLAMING WOMEN FOR MEN'S VIOLENCE

I want to be very clear about this: I am not surprised by the range and depth of acts of violence against women in the Australian Parliament that were revealed in the first months of 2021. Having researched this topic for over a decade, I am well acquainted with the ugly reality that violence against women permeates every corner of Australian life: it cuts across socioeconomic status, culture, age group, and yes, profession. However, I am somewhat shocked by how the public is only now appreciating the involvement of Australian parliamentarians in perpetrating, ignoring or excusing acts of sexual violence against women.

I am also shocked by the incredibly inadequate responses to these recent allegations. These may not be unique, but let's not lose sight of what they are: responses to alleged acts of violence against women from the highest levels of Australian government, from those with enormous platforms of power and influence. Our leaders should be held to a higher standard. In some instances, the response has entailed off-the-cuff remarks that demean the character of the victim. For example, an Australian Government minister described Brittany Higgins, an alleged rape victim, as a 'lying cow'.[10] Members of the media also have a case to answer: one radio presenter remarked, on air, that Higgins was 'a silly little girl who got drunk' and 'should have her bottom smacked'.[11]

Some denouncements have been more thought-out but just as poor, such as those speeches delivered by our nation's leaders to the media that have fallen drastically short of the leadership that is so desperately needed. For instance, speaking the day after the allegations made by Brittany Higgins first emerged, Prime Minister Morrison remarked:

> Jenny and I spoke last night and she said to me, 'You have to think about this as a father. What would you want to happen if it were our girls?' Jenny has a way of clarifying things. Always has.[12]

It's uncomfortable to imagine what it was that the Prime Minister was saying about the allegation and the woman involved that prompted his wife to ask him to reassess the situation with his own daughters in mind. The courageous Grace Tame, the 2021 Australian of the Year, who was groomed and repeatedly sexually assaulted by a teacher as a fifteen-year-old, was asked about Morrison's remark during a National Press Club address. She aptly responded: 'It shouldn't take having children to have a conscience. And, actually, on top of that, having children doesn't guarantee a conscience.'[13] Reponses like the Prime Minister's to victim-survivors of sexual violence are a stark reminder of just how intractable these attitudes are—views that dismiss the seriousness of violence against women and ultimately allow that violence to continue.

This behaviour is not unique to our political leaders, nor are the responses to these particular allegations. In the same week that Brittany Higgins first publicly described what she alleges happened to her, General Angus Campbell, Chief of the Australian Defence Force, told young cadets that the way to protect against sexual violence was to be aware of the 'Four As—alcohol, alone, attractive, and being out after midnight'.[14] This speaks directly to the problematic narrative surrounding men's violence in Australia: women must check their behaviour to avoid victimisation; the perpetrator, on the other hand, is not called to account or held responsible for his use of violence in the first instance.

Victim-blaming, which contributes to the lack of perpetrator accountability for violence against women, is an issue of profound significance for me. It is the reason that I embarked on a PhD in Criminology at Monash University in early 2008. I had enjoyed learning about the research process during my honours year, which came on the back of a three-year bachelor of arts degree where I first became interested in the field of criminology. But it was a niggling sense of injustice over one particular case that drove me to my PhD topic. Four years earlier, I—like many Victorians— had watched in disbelief and horror as James Ramage was convicted and sentenced to eleven years' jail for the manslaughter of his wife Julie. To me, the sentence seemed lenient given Ramage's lethal actions. But it was the highly problematic victim-blaming message sent by the court that struck me as most unjust, and which became a motivator for a significant portion of my career to date.

Let me take a step back here. In July 2003, Julie Ramage met with her estranged husband James at the previously shared family home in Melbourne to discuss renovation plans. Julie and James had been separated for five weeks following a twenty-year marriage. We only have James' version of events, put forward in his trial defence, to understand what happened during that meeting. He alleged that Julie dismissed the significance of the progress of the renovations, and that, responding to his plea that she return to the marriage, she told him that sex with him 'repulsed her and screwed up her face and either said or implied how much better her new [boy] friend was'.[15] James then claimed that he lost control and fatally attacked Julie in what was described by the judge as an act 'of immediate and overwhelming brutality by a man considerably larger and physically stronger than his victim'.[16]

There's a long list of facts and details that makes James Ramage's crime abhorrent, but I want to focus here on the injustice of the response by the courts. James did not deny that he had killed his wife. The trial concentrated on whether, in the time immediately prior to her death, Julie's actions had caused her estranged husband to lose his self-control and inflict lethal violence. Yes, it was *her* actions that were primarily given attention over the course of the trial.

Witnesses provided evidence of James' coercive and controlling behaviour throughout his marriage to Julie. These included acts of intimidation, forced sex, alleged physical violence and threats of violence.[17] The prosecution sought to use this evidence to demonstrate that Julie had held 'a continuing underlying fear' of

James, and that it was unlikely that she would have said the words attributed to her during the pair's final meeting.[18] Much of this evidence, however, was not heard by the jury. It was deemed highly prejudicial and subject to hearsay.[19] The evidence presented by the defence told a vastly different story.

James' defence sought to shift responsibility onto Julie by invoking victim-blaming gendered narratives. One argument by the defence counsel has stayed with me because it deftly illustrates all that is wrong not just with this case but with the way in which we blame women victims of intimate partner violence in Australia. The defence introduced evidence that Julie had tampons on her person at the time of her death to support their claim that she started the fatal argument with James. The Queen's Counsel representing James told the jury:

> Mrs Ramage was having her period, and you'll see in her handbag there were some tampons ... men tend to think that women get a bit scratchy at around that time—and if I'm wrong, dismiss it, okay? But Mrs Ramage went into that meeting, and according

to Mr Ramage, what happened was that she said hurtful things.[20]

Seventeen years later, I find these words, which belong to a bygone era but were spoken in a 21st-century Australian courtroom, just as appalling as when I first heard them. In her book examining the death of Julie Ramage, Karen Kissane remarks on this moment in the trial:

> Let's face it: who was it who was really having a bad day emotionally? Who was it who lost his temper in a murderous rage? Not the partner wearing a tampon … What is on trial here is not just Julie's sexual behaviour but female sexuality itself.[21]

Kissane is alluding to other evidence presented during the trial that sought to draw attention to the affairs Julie had had before and after her separation from her spouse and eventual killer. While James was presented as a successful businessman, a provider for his family, a husband grieving the breakdown of his marriage, Julie was painted as an unfaithful wife and a 'scratchy' woman.

Cases like this, where men kill women in the name of possession, are a sobering reminder of the patriarchal society that we continue to live in. Indeed, the time immediately following the dissolution of a relationship is recognised as a period of high risk when it comes to serious and fatal violence against women.[22] Julie Ramage is only one well-known tragedy among the numerous other Australian women who have been killed by the men they dared to leave.

At the end of the Ramage trial in the Victorian Supreme Court, the jury was invited to consider three possibilities: that James had murdered Julie; that he had acted without intent to kill and should be convicted of manslaughter; or that the prosecutors had failed to negate the partial defence of provocation and that he should be convicted of manslaughter on that ground. Ramage was subsequently convicted of manslaughter.

This was not justice. It is unacceptable for our criminal courts to be complicit in promulgating the idea that women bring about men's violence, that it is their responsibility and by extension their fault. When we blame women for men's violence, we utterly fail to hold men to account.

Since James Ramage's conviction for killing Julie, there has been significant reform across Australia of the partial defence of provocation, an archaic defence that serves to diminish the severity of the actions of *provoked* men.[23] Several states have abolished the partial defence entirely, while others have heavily restricted its application in a bid to ensure that it cannot be used in defence of the lethal actions of jealous men. And yet, despite this progress, I fear that similar victim-blaming narratives still emerge in different settings and institutions across our country. The beginning of 2021 offered a brutal reminder of this.

I find it outrageous that women are still routinely judged and condemned—as Rosie Batty felt she was all those years ago—for the violence committed against them. Whether they concern a grieving mother, a former Australian parliamentary staffer or the victim of a jealous husband, reactions to violence against women continue to focus on *how could she* as opposed to *how could he*: How could *she* let him do this? What did *she* do to cause that? The message is loud and clear: the women of Australia are responsible for the violence perpetrated against them by men.

THE EXTENT OF MEN'S VIOLENCE
AGAINST WOMEN

Whenever you focus on individual types of violence against women or high-profile cases, there is always the risk that you will fail to comprehend the over-all gravity of the problem of men's violence across Australia.

On average, at least one woman is killed by male violence each week in Australia.[24] According to Counting Dead Women, a brilliant volunteer community group that maintains a public register of women killed by men's violence in Australia, fifty-five women died in 2020 alone. This includes the high-profile February 2020 killing of Hannah Clarke and her three children, Aaliyah, Laianah and Trey—an unfathomable act that captured the country's attention and ignited a national debate about the risks of coercive and controlling behaviour.

At this year's March 4 Justice in Melbourne, a scroll of 868 names was unrolled in front of the stage, each name representing a woman killed by men's violence in Australia during the last ten years. There were names on the list that I knew well, from cases that I had researched in the field and from coverage in the media. But those I recognised were eclipsed by the ones I didn't know. Relatively few domestic homicides command national attention in this country. The harsh reality is that deaths like these are usually too commonplace to be considered newsworthy.

I appreciate the impracticality of the media covering every case of intimate partner homicide. And in some cases, keeping a crime out of the public spotlight may even be the wish of the victim's family and friends. But the silence surrounding some women's deaths when compared with the exposure received by others sits uncomfortably with me. Every woman's life matters.

In addition, when we focus only on deaths, we do not capture the full extent of the problems that lurk beneath. The prevalence of domestic, family and sexual violence is difficult to quantify given that acts of violence against women so often go unreported to the police—this applies to almost nine in ten incidents of sexual assault, according to a recent national survey.[25] When asked why they did not report such abuse, just over a third of the women respondents said they believed they could deal with the incident themselves, while another third said they did not regard the incident as a serious offence. Even more concerning, a quarter of the women cited feelings of shame or embarrassment as factors contributing to their unwillingness to go to the police. It is a dire reflection of contemporary community attitudes that the majority of women still carry the burden of shame for the sexually violent actions of men.

Silence and shame as barriers to reporting are not unique to sexual violence. Almost half of the women who experience violence from a current or former intimate partner do not seek any advice or support, and over 80 per cent never contact the police to report that violence.[26] These statistics are even more alarming when you consider that, Australia-wide, police respond to a family or domestic violence incident every two minutes.[27] Despite these high numbers, in too many instances, that call is never made.

Keeping those caveats around under-reporting in mind, consider what is known about the frequency of different forms of violence against women. One of the more reliable prevalence estimates we have is the Australian Bureau of Statistics' Personal Safety Survey, which provides a national overview of the violence experienced by Australians aged fifteen years and older, specifically in the twelve months immediately prior to the survey. According to the latest findings:

- one in six women has experienced physical or sexual violence by a current or previous partner since the age of fifteen, which is equal to 1.6 million Australian women

- one in four women has experienced emotional abuse by a current or previous partner since the age of fifteen, which is equal to 2.2 million Australian women

- one in six women was physically or sexually abused before they were fifteen years old, which is equal to 1.5 million Australian women.[28]

While the sordid allegations of sexual violence that have emerged from within the walls of Parliament House have shocked many, for the one in six Australian women who have experienced sexual violence, they may come as no surprise.

Sexual assault is the most common form of sexual violence reported in Australia. This umbrella term is used to describe a range of sexually violent behaviours, including rape. According to the Personal Safety Survey, Australian women are most likely to be sexually assaulted by a person known to them—typically their intimate partner—in their home, often with the involvement of alcohol or other drugs.[29]

The national prevalence rates of violence against women have remained stable over the past ten years. You could take some solace in the fact that they have not risen in that time, but it is incredibly frustrating to me that, despite some efforts—particularly at the state and territory level—we have yet to demonstrate measurable progress towards reduction and prevention. We can't be satisfied with this plateau. Women in Australia deserve a much greater degree of safety and a concerted drive towards the elimination of the violence routinely committed against them.

While domestic and family violence is present across *all* Australian communities, there are some groups that are impacted more heavily than others,

KATE FITZ-GIBBON

and some women who face a greater risk of violence. Aboriginal and Torres Strait Islander women
experience all forms of family and domestic violence
at significantly higher rates than non-Indigenous
Australians. Aboriginal women are twice as likely to
be killed by an intimate partner than non-Aboriginal
women, and they are up to thirty-two times more
likely to be hospitalised as a result of domestic and
family violence.[30] Every time I read these statistics
I am confounded by the everyday violent reality of
Aboriginal women's lives.

As a white Australian woman, I also feel ashamed
and complicit, as I know that the colonial brutality in our history has a lot to answer for here. At
March 4 Justice, I listened to the powerful words
of Sue-Anne Hunter, a Wurundjeri woman, social
worker and advocate who is committed to improving
the rights of Aboriginal children and families:

Aboriginal women have fought against gendered
violence perpetrated by white men since day one.
The allegations, cover up and silence on gendered
violence in federal parliament is part of the same

system of abuse and the same lack of legal and political consequences. Enough is Enough.[31]

The push over the last three decades to toughen criminal justice system responses to men's violence against women has exacerbated these harms. Strategies to criminalise violence against women have had disproportionate impacts on Aboriginal and Torres Strait Islander communities, which are over-policed and their members over-imprisoned.[32] All the while there has been ongoing silence from those in leadership on the violence that Indigenous women routinely experience. As Professor Bronwyn Carlson recently wrote, it is both 'normalised and rendered invisible'.[33]

There are no easy solutions, but it is very clear that the current approach is not working—and that it hasn't been working for a very long time. Community interventions need to be led by Indigenous people and must be culturally sensitive. Indigenous voices must be heard and privileged, and those in power must listen and learn. Importantly, those who have the political power to do so must direct the required resources to

Indigenous communities so that they can themselves drive the prevention and response interventions needed to meaningfully and appropriately address all forms of domestic, family and sexual violence.

BEYOND THE FAMILY

I have focused so far on women's experience of violence by their male partners, and deliberately so. Intimate partner violence is the most prevalent form of violence against women.[34] It is not an outlier, though, as men's violence is all too common in a multitude of settings within and beyond the home.

Given the allegations with which this book began, it seems appropriate to start with the workplace. Kate Jenkins, Australia's Sex Discrimination Commissioner, has described the progress being made in preventing and addressing sexual harassment in the workplace as 'disappointingly slow'. She is being polite in doing so. Her own report, which was compiled under the auspices of the Australian Human Rights Commission, *Respect@Work*, reveals that one in three people have experienced sexual harassment at their workplace in the past five years—this equates to two in five Australian women and just over one in four Australian men.[35] While the majority of incidents are never publicly disclosed and are unlikely to be settled in the courts, a review of case law in this area reveals the range of harms that can be included under the banner of sexual harassment. They include cases where:

A law firm boss appears in the bedroom of a junior female employee during a work trip dressed only in his underwear. An IT company sales representative tells a colleague he will be thinking about her legs 'wrapped around me all day long'. A construction worker tells a female co-worker: 'I am going to follow you home, rip your clothes off and rape you'.[36]

Unsurprisingly, the rate of sexual harassment increases in male-dominated workplaces (construction and mining, for example). It also increases in organisations that have clear hierarchal structures (the police, the medical and legal professions), and where workers have a high level of contact with clients, customers or patients (retail, the hospitality and health sectors).[37]

The Me Too and Times Up movements have played a key role in shining a light into the darkest corners of some industries and workplaces. But while they have been responsible for some high-profile achievements, I suspect there is still much to uncover that requires redress. I like to think that, as they see the power of women such as Brittany Higgins, there are many men sitting nervously in their offices around the country, wondering: When will my time be up? When will my actions be exposed?

And perhaps that time is edging closer. In April 2021, some thirteen months after the AHRC presented its landmark report on sexual harassment in the Australian workplace, the Morrison government committed itself in principle to adopting the report's fifty-five recommendations, which will be critical in addressing unsafe workplace policies and practices. That the government sat on this report for over a year is frustrating to say the very least, but there is now some hope of traction—although, of course, the devil will be in the detail, and in the extent to which that traction translates into meaningful action.

It would be remiss of me not to say something here about 'stranger danger'. It is instilled in numerous children—certainly in young girls—that strange men are generally to be feared and are to be avoided whenever possible, especially at night. While it is inaccurate to say there is no threat here, the risk an Australian woman faces from a stranger is much lower than the risk she faces in her own home, from a man she knows and trusts. The killing of women by a stranger or by someone whom they have just met accounts for 3 per cent of homicides in Australia.[38] It is an extremely rare event.

Still, when they do occur, these killings often capture the public's attention in a way that rarely happens with domestic homicides, with the exception of a small number of high-profile cases. The women's names are etched into the public vernacular: Jill Meagher, Eurydice Dixon, Masa Vukotic, Aiia Maasarwe—all Victorian incidents, each woman killed by a man unknown to her while walking home. The cases are unrelated and occurred years apart, but the names of these women have become inextricably linked because of the everyday activity they were each undertaking when attacked, and the horrific nature of their deaths. As retired Supreme Court judge Frank Vincent said in the case of Jill Meagher, 'She was a young woman, simply going about engaging in ordinary activity and died in that process'.[39]

Many will recall the CCTV footage released by Victoria Police shortly after the disappearance of Jill Meagher in the Melbourne suburb of Brunswick in late September 2012. Taken from inside a bridal store, it showed a man—whom we now know as the serial rapist and murderer Adrian Bayley—walking first in one direction along the sidewalk, then back the other way, before again appearing onscreen walking slightly ahead of but turned towards a woman: Jill. The scene in and of itself is ordinary; there are no signs of the life-ending violence that was to follow. But the video's public release accompanied by a plea for assistance, four days after Jill had disappeared, was significant in focusing attention on the case—Bayley would be arrested two days later.

CCTV footage also allegedly played a key role in the confession of Eurydice Dixon's killer in 2018, almost six years after Jill Meagher's death. The circumstances were all too familiar: a woman walking home at night, in this case after performing a comedy show at a Melbourne bar, and being killed by a young man previously unknown to her. The details of the case are chilling. Jaymes Todd followed Eurydice Dixon on foot for over an hour before killing her, walking for 4 kilometres through inner Melbourne. In her powerful essay on the topic, Sarah Krasnostein describes Todd's thoughts during this predatory hour as contemplating 'the fantasy in which he has invested so much time and emotion: a fantasy in which he is always in control and in which the other person is always female, raped then killed'.[40] While a statistical rarity, this is nonetheless the stuff of nightmares.

For so many women, the fear instilled by these deaths has influenced their behaviour when using public spaces. Yet, as with the violence that occurs within our homes, it is still women who are assigned the responsibility to maintain their own safety. This was demonstrated by the comments made by the head of the Victoria Police homicide squad, detective inspector Mick Hughes, in 2015 following the day-time killing of seventeen-year-old Masa Vukotic in a Melbourne park by Sean Price. Speaking on radio, Hughes offered this advice: 'I suggest to people, particularly females, [that] they shouldn't be alone in parks. I'm sorry to say that that is the case. We just need to be a little more careful, a little more security conscious.'[41]

The focus here is entirely unsatisfactory—the actions of a young woman walking on her own in a public park during the daytime. Adopting Hughes' own words here, should we not perhaps suggest to people, particularly men, that they shouldn't kill women? I'm sorry to say that that is the case. We just need men to be a little more careful, a little less murderous.

Perpetrator accountability matters, but when we focus on the behaviour of the victim, we do so at the expense of holding the perpetrator to account. Some leaders, at least, have correctly recognised that it is not women who should be modifying their actions. Victorian Premier Dan Andrews, for example, said following the killing of Eurydice Dixon: 'Our message to Victorian women is this: stay home. Or don't. Go out with friends at night. Or don't. Go about your day exactly as you intend, on your terms.'[42]

What leaders in the community say about these issues is important because it guides and informs the conversations that follow, as well as how we understand the act that has been committed and where responsibility for it lies. Yet all too often we have had to rely on the informal leadership of women to demand that the right message is heard. In the aftermath of several of the killings I have mentioned here, women took to the streets to 'Reclaim the night'. This movement started in the late 1970s in the United Kingdom, Continental Europe and the United States and has since spread further afield. It represents moments in time when women have reclaimed their right to personal safety, to walk without fear.[43] The power of coming together to do so is symbolic—women unite in their fight for the right to be safe in public spaces; they unite in their commitment to end violence perpetrated against them.

At the individual level, one of the most powerful statements about the killing of Jill Meagher came from her husband, Tom Meagher. Reflecting on the moment that he heard Bayley speak in court, Tom wrote:

> I had formed an image that this man was not human, that he existed as a singular force of pure evil who somehow emerged from the ether. Something about his ability to weave together nouns, verbs and pronouns to form real, intelligible sentences forced a re-focus, one that required a look at the spectrum of men's violence against women, and its relation to Bayley and the society from which he came. By insulating myself with the intellectually evasive dismissal of violent men as psychotic or sociopathic aberrations, I self-comforted by avoiding the more terrifying concept that violent men are socialised by the ingrained sexism and entrenched masculinity that permeates everything from our daily interactions all the way up to our highest institutions.
>
> Bayley's appeal was dismissed, but I left court that day in a perpetual trauma-loop, knowing I needed to re-imagine the social, institutional and cultural context in which a man like Adrian Bayley exists.[44]

For me, Tom Meagher's reflections eloquently confront the reality that gender inequalities and disrespect towards women in our community underpin the violent actions of men such as Adrian Bayley. I was fortunate to spend some time with Tom at a conference in the beautiful Irish city of Cork a few years back; he had moved back to Ireland and was working in the violence-against-women sector. He was incredibly insightful on the root causes of violence against women, which unsurprisingly had nothing to do with the actions of the victims themselves. Tom's conference presentation encouraged a better understanding of the problematic cultures within our society that allow men's violence to thrive.

WHAT ABOUT MEN?

Perhaps this is the point at which to address the question I inevitably get asked, and which is also asked of media commentators on this issue: 'What about men?' I have no doubt that I will hear it again in relation to a book that is subtitled 'Violence against Women', which is unapologetically my focus.

I find this question frustrating. Despite being presented with overwhelming evidence as to the disproportionate levels of violence and death that women in Australia face in comparison to their male counterparts, there are sceptics who endeavour to dilute the focus on women by questioning whether men, too, are being victimised. More often than not, asking 'What about men?' can be an unhelpful attempt to change the gendered conversation on domestic, family and sexual violence. The fact of the matter is that adult men in Australia are not victimised at anywhere near the same rate as women. While men do experience all forms of family, domestic and sexual violence, they do so less frequently and with less fatal outcomes.

While acknowledging that men's experiences of family, domestic and sexual violence—like those of women—are often likely unreported, the research tells us that:

- one in sixteen men have experienced physical or sexual violence by a current or previous partner since the age of fifteen

- one in six men have experienced emotional abuse by a current or previous partner since the age of fifteen
- one in twenty men have experienced sexual violence since the age of fifteen
- one in nine men were physically or sexually abused before the age of fifteen.[45]

These are certainly not insignificant numbers. For men in the community who do experience family, domestic and sexual violence, the effort of seeking help can be met with significant barriers, such as a lack of services specifically for men, a lack of online options, and a lack of knowledge in the community as to what support is available. Men who experience family and domestic violence also report feeling shame, that they are disbelieved, or that their experience of violence is not taken seriously.[46]

It is true that the unmet need here for men is nowhere near as great as it is for women, and that the problem to be addressed is not as widespread. But of course we cannot tolerate violence anywhere in our community—to turn a blind eye to violence, wherever it arises, is irresponsible. We need appropriate and accessible services for all the members of our community who experience violence.

THE IMPACT OF MEN'S VIOLENCE AGAINST WOMEN

The sheer number of women who experience domestic, family and sexual violence in any one year in Australia is so great that it can be easy to forget that the figure is made up of individuals, each one a woman whose life will have been heavily impacted by that experience of violence. The effects can be serious and long-lasting, eroding her physical and mental health, education and employment opportunities, housing, and her relationships with family and friends.

A few years back, I attended the launch of a Victorian study into the role of family violence in cases of acquired brain injury. The hallmarks of physically abusive relationships, such as trauma to the head and strangulation, unsurprisingly cause such injuries. Utilising hospital data, the study found that 40 per cent of family violence victims who attended a Victorian hospital between 2006 and 2016 had sustained damage to the brain.[47] People who have been injured in this way may require income, housing, education or parenting support, and may have an impeded capacity to recover from the abuse they have suffered. This is yet another way in which men's violence impacts the day-to-day lives, and the futures, of those who experience it.

In Australia, family and domestic violence is also the leading cause of homelessness for women.[48] A national study conducted in 2016–17 found that, over a twelve-month period, approximately 72 000 women, 34 000 children and 9000 men sought help from homelessness services, citing domestic and family violence as a contributor to their housing needs.[49] It beggars belief that in a single year, in a country as seemingly fortunate as Australia, over 100 000 people can be driven into housing instability due to domestic and family violence.

It is important to keep this in mind when the inevitable question of 'Why doesn't she just leave?' is voiced, as it so often is. Frequently, leaving is not a viable option for women. You may as well ask, 'Why didn't she keep herself safe?' Yet again we see how the responsibility for personal wellbeing is placed on the victim, while the perpetrator avoids responsibility for the violence they inflict.

When we talk about the impact of men's violence on a female partner, it is often what is difficult to see and readily describe that has the most devastating consequences. The everyday risk of violence within coercive and controlling relationships can be difficult to fully comprehend from an outside perspective.

Coercive control is a term that has a long history in clinical settings.[50] It refers to a broad pattern of behaviours that include social, financial, psychological and technology-facilitated abuse. Isolating a person from their friends and family, restricting their movements, controlling their appearance or access to money, using tracking devices to monitor their phone—it is often the independence of the victim that is targeted. Coercive control has more recently risen up political agendas across Australia courtesy of debates about whether it should be introduced as a criminal offence. I have been heavily involved in those debates, and while I don't want to talk here about the merits or otherwise of making this behaviour a

specific crime, I do want to impart the terror con-
tinually suffered by women in coercively controlled
relationships. There are often no bruises, no physical
marks in evidence, but a woman's interior being, her
sense of self and ability to lead an independent life,
can be dramatically affected.

In Australia, as elsewhere around the world, there
is a push for the term 'coercive control' to be more
widely used, to ensure full recognition of the patterns
of abuse faced by women experiencing intimate
partner violence. Decades of focusing on individual
incidents of physical violence have, many argue,
impeded a full appreciation of the patterns of men's
violence. When we do not see the complete picture,
we cannot appreciate its true nature and full impact.

Recently, as part of the NSW Parliamentary Joint
Select Committee on Coercive Control, a discussion
paper was released by the NSW Government.[51] The
paper draws on the work of Evan Stark to describe
coercive control as a:

> pattern of domination and control that is created
> through a collection of behaviours. These behaviours

may include physical, sexual, psychological, financial and emotional abuse and intimidation, used as tactics by a perpetrator to gain power, control and dominance over the victim-survivor. Coercive control is typically an interwoven course of conduct carried out over time. Individual acts may appear trivial, whilst forming part of a broader matrix of abusive behaviours that serve to reinforce and strengthen the control and dominance of one person over another.[52]

This description of the behaviours that are included under the banner of coercive control effectively conveys the awful day-to-day reality for women who live within abusive relationships of this nature. We know that this form of family violence is unfortunately all too common for women in Australia. The NSW Domestic Violence Death Review Team has found that coercive and controlling behaviours were perpetrated in a relationship prior to over 90 per cent of the intimate partner homicides that occurred between 2008 and 2016.[53] The team's work clearly highlights how coercive control cannot be dismissed as merely non-physical acts of violence, as acts that do not threaten the day-to-day wellbeing and safety of Australian women.

The fatal consequences of a coercive and controlling relationship occupied the public conscience following the horrific killing of Hannah Clarke and her three children. Hannah's estranged husband, Rowan Baxter, ambushed his ex-partner when she was driving her three children to school from the Brisbane suburb of Camp Hill on the morning of 19 February 2020. Baxter dowsed the interior of the family car in petrol and a short time later set it alight, killing Aaliyah, Laianah and Trey. Hannah died that afternoon from injuries she sustained in the attack.[54] Baxter killed himself at the scene of the fire.

Since her death, it has been reported that Hannah experienced years of coercive and controlling behaviour by her then husband. Sue Clarke has recounted what her daughter endured:

> He always knew where Hannah was, he would turn up at places quite unexpectedly, and she would notice her handbag or phone had been rifled through.

He would ring her when she should be locking up the gym, to see if she had locked up on time and if there was anyone there with her. He would control what she wore. Hannah was never allowed to wear pink or shorts ... He would also control what the children did, and he would force sex on Hannah every night and if she didn't comply he would sulk for days.[55]

What Sue Clarke is describing here are the controlling behaviours all too commonly experienced by women in abusive intimate partner relationships. These are among the tactics used by abusive men to gain full control over the lives of their partners, to whittle away at their sense of independence. As the death of Hannah Clarke so brutally shows, we need to better understand such behaviours as the key warning sign that a woman is at risk of serious injury or death.

At the time of her killing, Hannah had a civil protection order in place against her estranged husband—Baxter had been charged with breaching the order weeks before and was due to appear in court. Hannah had even met with a former police officer to work out a security plan.[56] I remember reading these details of Hannah's life and sensing absolute despair—here was a woman who had so desperately tried to protect her children and herself, with numerous professionals aware of the risk that Baxter posed, and yet she had been killed. The deaths of Hannah, Aaliyah, Laianah and Trey prove how much work is still to be done to stop the violence being perpetrated by men.

A STAGGERING COST

Beyond the individual impact, at the community level, the price of men's violence against women is staggering. In 2016, the United Nations estimated that this costs the global economy US$1.5 trillion annually.[57] In regards to Australia, the 2020 Women's Economic Security Statement noted that violence against women and their children costs the economy $26 billion every year.[58] Almost 50 per cent of this— $10.4 billion—is attributed to the costs borne by victim-survivors, reflecting how they are at increased risk of chronic illness and pain, and reproductive health problems. Within this total national expense, workplace sexual harassment is estimated to cost the economy $3.5 billion annually,[59] with $2.6 billion accorded to the lost productivity that occurs as a result.[60] This includes the toll of absenteeism as well as that of increased staff turnover and pressure on managerial time.

When we compare the costs that the community bears as a result of violence against women with the funding dedicated at the federal level to address this wicked problem, the imbalance is mind-boggling. The 2020 Women's Economic Security Statement, which is produced by the Australian Government, proudly notes that $1 billion has been invested annually by the government to respond to and prevent violence against women and their children since 2013.[61] While the initial price tag sounds impressive, it equates to $1 billion dedicated over a seven-year period to addressing a problem that costs the economy over three times that amount in a single year.

It is also difficult to isolate what proportion of the available money is directly targeting violence against women, both in terms of dedicated funding for front-line responses and ongoing support for prevention efforts. The 2020 Budget allocated $240 million over five years for enhancing women's financial security and participation in paid work, which, when contextualised, accounts for 0.04 per cent of the total budget outgoings. To put this another way, it means that 0.038 per cent of the national budget was allocated to ensuring the economic security and personal safety of 51 per cent of the Australian population. Shortly after the budget announcement, the journalist and gender-equality advocate Georgie Dent commented that women's security issues 'are significant and the suggestion that they could be even marginally improved by spending less than one percent of the entire Budget is absolute fantasy at best'.[62]

The 2020 Budget also lacked additional funding for addressing violence against women. Yes, that is correct. In the midst of a pandemic that disproportionately affected the economic and personal safety of women across the globe,[63] including in Australia,[64] the federal government declined to use the budget to up its commitment to keeping women safe.

The 2020 Budget is not an anomaly. In 2016, my Monash colleagues and I wrote an article for *The Age* calling out the higher priority given in the federal budget to terrorism over violence against women.[65] In that year's budget, the government allocated $100 million over three years to domestic and family violence–related items. In comparison, $30 billion was directed to national security, with the promise of 'keeping Australians safe' from terrorism threats abroad.[66] Of course, countering threats to national security must be a priority for the federal government, but the disparity in funding is unexplainable and inexcusable. In any given year over the last decade, more than twice as many women have been killed by their male intimate partners (current and former) than people killed in Australia as a result of terrorism offences since 2001.[67] I feel ongoing frustration at the willingness of politicians to ignore the reality of where Australians most require protection.

Some people are quick to categorise violence against women as a social issue, but equally it is a hugely important economic issue for our country. Investing in women's safety has widespread, long-term benefits for the Australian economy. Research in Australia and overseas has consistently found that women who are financially independent are better positioned to leave an abusive male partner, and to remain separated from them in the long term.[68] Financial security also increases the likelihood that a person can recover from the devastating impacts of domestic and family violence. Yet time and time again we do not see these perspectives reflected in the budgets announced by our federal parliament.

Politicians are yet to release a budget that takes women's safety seriously. This is urgently needed to maintain women's long-term safety, in turn allowing them to thrive.

A SHADOW PANDEMIC

What about COVID-19? To what extent has the pandemic necessitated a change in how we understand and respond to all forms of violence against women?

Shortly after the outbreak of the virus, the Executive Director of United Nations Women,

Phumzile Mlambo-Ngcuka, labelled violence against women the 'shadow pandemic'.[69] The declaration was useful as it provided a label to describe what many, including myself, already feared: that family, domestic and sexual violence would be exacerbated during the pandemic. This was a concern shared globally.

In early April 2020, as the virus rapidly spread and countries worldwide entered into varying degrees of government-enforced lockdown, the United Nations Population Fund predicted that for every three months of such lockdowns, an additional 15 million cases of domestic violence would occur globally.[70] Yes, 15 million *additional* cases. As we negotiate the second year of the pandemic, with government-enforced restrictions still commonplace internationally and occasional in Australia, it is confronting to consider the vast number of women who have recently experienced violence at home for the first time, and the women for whom violence has increased in severity and frequency.

Keep in mind that, several years ago, the United Nations declared the home as the most dangerous place for women worldwide.[71] The degree to which women's safety has now been further eroded during the pandemic is almost unfathomable.

This is not to suggest that coronavirus is, in and of itself, a cause of violence against women. Absolutely not—the responsibility here lies firmly with the men who choose to use violence, and the gender inequality that persists across our community. But the COVID-19 pandemic has certainly aggravated the conditions within which men's violence flourishes. During the periods of lockdown, deemed necessary from a public health perspective, women and children have been isolated more than ever before, access to formal and informal supports have been minimised, and financial stress has increased.[72] The resultant mental health stresses levied on individuals and their families cannot be underestimated.[73]

When the federal government's first COVID-19 restrictions were announced in March 2020, and then again as we rolled through varying stages of restrictions in Victoria throughout the rest of that year, I was ever conscious of the dire circumstances of the many women who were being forced to isolate at home with their abusers, and the irony of the government's 'Stay home, stay safe' mantra.

GENDER INEQUALITY AND MISOGYNY

So what causes violence against women? The answer is strikingly simple: men. But what if we ask ourselves a different question? What if we ask what causes men to choose to use violence against the women in their lives? And let's be clear here—it is a choice, one that far too many men across Australia make on a daily basis. In 2015, then prime minister Malcolm Turnbull said, 'Not all disrespect of women ends in violence, but all violence begins with disrespect'.[74] He could not have been more on point. The fundamental cause of violence against women in this country—and indeed globally—is gender inequality, which breeds a disrespect and a disregard for women.

Gender inequality is not a vague or abstract concept. It is a real-life limitation that we can point to in the everyday experiences of women and girls across Australia. The national gender pay gap, for example, stands at 13.9 per cent.[75] Gender inequality is the extra hours, days or indeed weeks that a woman is required to work to earn the same salary as her male counterpart. It means that women in Australia retire with significantly less superannuation than men and consequently are at greater risk of living in poverty or facing homelessness in their later years.

I recently revisited prime minister Julia Gillard's iconic 2012 'misogyny speech', as it has come to be known. Reading it in 2021 is both a cause of panic and simultaneously one of calm. Gillard so clearly articulates the problem of misogyny, hence the calm: if we know what the problem is, then surely we can address it. But the panic sets in upon the realisation that so much of the content of her speech still resonates today. The misogyny that she identified as being characteristic of the culture of Australia's national parliament has not been ameliorated since her powerful stand almost a decade ago. Indeed, many fear that it has only worsened.

In her speech, Gillard implored the then leader of the Opposition, Tony Abbott, to 'think seriously about the role of women in public life and in

Australian society because we are entitled to a better standard than this'.[76] This remains a requirement of our parliamentarians, on both sides of the aisle. Gillard was right in saying that, if the leaders of our country—both male and female—who have a platform from which to speak cannot take responsibility for their own sexist and misogynistic actions, then what hope do we have that those same leaders will lead the national change we need on this issue?

The endemic hatred of and prejudice against women that we have seen in the Australian Parliament and across the country's political scene in recent months—and let's be honest here: over the years—highlights the significance of the task ahead. And while the early months of 2021 have seen women march in their thousands and take to podiums across the country to demand an end to misogynistic leadership, behaviours and processes, we are fooling ourselves if we think this problem is unique to the current year. In 2019, Dr Anne Summers, a leading Australian feminist and writer, said in a speech at the National Press Club:

The Liberal Party has a man problem. And a merit problem. And a misogyny problem. And all three of these 'M's are inextricably connected ... Misogyny, which I define as hostility to women, is expressed by wanting them excluded from places—be they boardrooms, or conclaves, or political parties—where decisions are made about the kind of country we are and can be ... misogyny is now the hallmark of the Liberal Party. It is a badge worn with pride and it is not going to be surrendered.[77]

But while the problem has resisted a widespread solution for some time now, perhaps we have reached the point where we can finally get the traction that has been so desperately sought after in years past. We must be prepared to confront the fact that the attitudes that underpin misogynistic actions also underpin the very worst violence that men perpetrate against women. For a long time, women have understood this correlation, and while it is a far more complex and long-term problem to address than many realise, women *and* men must commit to doing so. Our efforts must be concentrated on dealing with attitudinal misogyny and widespread gender inequalities as the drivers of violence against women in Australia.

Leading academics have referred to a continuum of violence.[78] While men's violence against women can take many different forms—be it physical, coercive and controlling, sexualised, intimidatory, or focused on property or pets, for example—all of these are underpinned and linked by the male desire for power and control over women. We can see this in the seemingly random acts of male violence perpetrated by the likes of Adrian Bayley and Jaymes Todd, but also in the targeted actions of men who are violent towards the women they profess to love. It is not surprising that the breakdown of a relationship and the period of separation immediately following this is a time of incredible risk for women. It is when women attempt to assert their independence, when they attempt to live an individual life, when *his* control over her is at threat, that they are at the greatest risk of serious, all too often fatal violence.

It is that same lust for power and control, that same deep-seated disrespect for women, that also determines the indirect actions that men take against the women in their lives. The killing of a child by their father, for example, has been attributed as an act of revenge against the mother. This is thought to have been the case with Arthur Freeman, who was convicted of the 2009 murder of his four-year-old daughter Darcey in Melbourne. Chief Crown prosecutor Gavin Silbert SC submitted at trial that Freeman was solely and entirely motivated by a desire for spousal revenge.[79] By tackling the misogynistic motivations of men who use violence, we can reduce the violence committed against women and their children, and even, eventually, prevent it altogether.

A PREVENTABLE CRISIS

To understand the root causes of men's violence against women is to begin to identify a pathway towards prevention and ultimately elimination. In this respect, while I do not underestimate the magnitude of the task involved, violence against women should be understood as a preventable problem.

My research into acts of femicide—the killing of a woman—committed both in Australia and overseas over the last decade has cemented this idea for me. Women's deaths from male violence are preventable; I have noticed this time and time again. In some cases, they are preventable because the systemic failings that contributed to a woman's death are identifiable and *should* be rectifiable. In other cases, they are preventable by virtue of the number of known risk factors present in the victim's life prior to the act of femicide. All too often, when I look back through the lives of the women killed by men's violence, the number of different services and systems that had only a partial perspective on the woman or the male become apparent. Piecemeal reform and siloed responses fail to allow the full picture of men's violence and the risks women face to be brought into view.

I am reminded here of the killing of Kelly Thompson in Victoria in February 2014 by her former partner, Wayne Wood.[80] In the months before her death, Kelly had taken out an intervention order against Wood that had been breached on at least two occasions, and Wood had also repeatedly threatened violence against Kelly, along with incidents where he stalked and tried to strangle her. In the three weeks before she was killed, Kelly called the police on at least thirty-five occasions and also disclosed the violence to friends, neighbours and work colleagues. Only a few hours before she was killed, Kelly's neighbour called the police to report that Wood was at Kelly's house and acting strangely; he also told the police that he believed Wood was in breach of an intervention order. But the police officer who took that call did not check to see if there was an intervention order in place, nor did he send police to the house. Instead, the officer asked the neighbour: 'Can you do me a massive favour pal and keep an eye on the address? If you hear any yelling or screaming from the address, I'll send a van around to have a look.'[81]

Recalling that response elicits the same reaction in me every time. Is this really the best we can do? Three hours after her neighbour contacted the police, Kelly was stabbed to death and Wood committed suicide. Another woman killed by men's violence; another woman who tried desperately to get help.

The coronial inquest held into Kelly's death perhaps unsurprisingly found that police oversights meant that serious threats to Thompson's safety were not recognised or acted upon. While the coroner was careful not to imply that anyone but Wayne Wood was responsible for Kelly Thompson's death, he did find that the police response 'fell short' and pointed to the absence of a proper risk assessment, a lack of police understanding of intimate partner violence, a number of missed opportunities to intervene, and the limitations of information-sharing provisions between police and family violence agencies.[82]

For me, the circumstances surrounding Kelly's death so clearly capture many of the failings in our family violence system, particularly around comprehensive responses and the need for effective risk assessment and management practices. While Kelly Thompson was killed over seven years ago, many of these weaknesses in system responses to family violence remain across Australia's states and territories.

While I point here to failings of justice system agencies in keeping women safe, I must stress that we will not be able to arrest or jail our way out of this problem. And we cannot focus our attention on the quick wins that criminal justice reform provides. While there is a role for agencies such as the police, courts and corrections, it must be viewed as a contained and inherently limited one. The criminal justice system is a blunt tool, and by nature it is reactive, not preventative. If we wait until women call the police or police intervention is required, then we are quite simply accepting that women will experience intimate partner violence. We are resigning ourselves to always becoming involved after the fact. What I am calling for here is a commitment to prevention and to the elimination of violence against women—there will always be a need for an effective and well-funded response system, but we must ensure it does not come at the cost of investing in prevention.

Regarding this goal of prevention, all Australians have a part to play in improving women's safety and freedom from men's violence—family, friends, neighbours and work colleagues. This means no more bystanders. As I write this, the organisation Our Watch has launched the second phase of its 'Doing nothing does harm' campaign. The message is clear: all members of the Australian community must act when they see or hear disrespectful actions towards women.

The consequences of inaction, of merely being a bystander, were clearly illustrated to me on 16 April 2020. I can remember standing in my kitchen after another work-from-home day, speaking on the phone to my Monash colleague Silke Meyer after seeing a news item on the killing of yet another Australian woman. This was during Victoria's first lockdown, and my peers and I were spending many hours each day examining what the COVID-19 restrictions would mean for the women and children experiencing domestic and family violence. On that day, South Australian Police had discovered the body of Kim Murphy in her Adelaide home. Initial investigations revealed that, the previous night, several neighbours had heard disturbances at the property, including a threat to kill, and the mother crying for help.[83] But no-one called the police.

Kim's former male partner was charged by the police with murder. The investigating officer, detective superintendent Des Bray, said:

It is a sad reflection on society that people would hear that and not ring the police. I'm at a complete loss to understand why anybody wouldn't do something and go to the aid or ensure that somebody went to the aid of a woman who was screaming for help.[84]

The death of Kim Murphy and the comments from Bray underline the critical role of onlookers, as well as the potential for well-informed bystander interventions, in saving the lives of Australian women and preventing future acts of violence. To date, however, very little has been invested in this space beyond advertising campaigns, which are merely one piece of the puzzle.

For many women and children experiencing violence, it is their family, friends, neighbours and/or co-workers who first become aware of their victimisation. For example, recent national survey data on sexual violence reveals that of those women who were subjected to such violence, just over 70 per cent sought help from a friend or family member.[85] Likewise, in regards to victims of intimate partner violence, 65 per cent sought advice or support from a friend or family member. While we often focus on system and specialist service responses, these results clearly highlight the value and importance of informal networks.

Bystanders represent an early point of possible intervention, and critically, an early opportunity to connect victims with the relevant support services and to engage in safety planning. But all too often, family and friends do not know what specifically to say or do, and they are paralysed by that uncertainty into doing or saying nothing. This must change.

DEAFENING SILENCE: THE LACK OF NATIONAL LEADERSHIP

The lack of meaningful action and leadership at the federal level regarding violence against women can no longer be ignored, excused or explained away. The relative silence from Canberra on this issue reflects a legacy of national leadership that has never taken women's safety seriously.

In early 2016, when Rosie Batty finished her time as Australian of the Year, she remarked:

In my acceptance speech last year, I said that family violence may happen behind closed doors, but it needed to be brought out from the shadows and into broad daylight. I pledged that as the Australian of the Year I was committed to building greater campaigns to educate and challenge community attitudes ... I am so proud to stand here to say that I have done what I set out to do. I believe that we, as a nation, have made great progress over the last twelve months. The conversation has not only started, it is now well underway ... whilst Family Violence is still happening behind closed doors, the conversations aren't. We are now having deep, confronting conversations, the ones we really need to have. In the home, workplace, and amongst our political parties. We are shifting the blame previously placed on to the victim and re-directing it to where it squarely needs to be, to the perpetrators of this violence. And that is the significant progress that I am very proud of.[86]

Five years later, however, we are still confronting the same daily reality of violence against women.

There have undoubtedly been small achievements, and family violence is certainly now part of the national conversation. But the change we ultimately need, a deep-seated change in community attitudes and gender inequality, is proving stubbornly slow to materialise. Rosie should feel a sense of pride about what she was able to achieve in her role as Australian of the Year; indeed, to me, she has been the absolute stand-out individual in this role in my lifetime. However, her hopes for what those conversations would lead to are as yet unrealised. The 'deep, confronting conversations' she noted have not led to the redirection of responsibility that she sought.

Interestingly, when reflecting on the question 'So, what is it we must do?' in her powerful address to the National Press Club in March 2021, Grace Tame returned to the focus of her Australian of the Year predecessor, Rosie Batty:

First and foremost, let's keep talking about it. It's that simple. Let's start by opening up. It is up to us as a community, as a country, to create a space, a national movement where survivors feel supported and free to share their truths. Let's drive a paradigm shift of shame away from those who have been abused and onto abusive behaviour ... Certainly, talking about child sexual abuse won't eradicate it, but we can't fix a problem we don't discuss, so it begins with conversation.[87]

Grace's call for greater community awareness, and a supportive environment in which the expertise and experience of victim-survivors is privileged and heard, is an essential step towards transformational change at the federal level. I'd like to push it one step further: we also need a whole-of-community—indeed, a whole-of-country—action plan for the elimination of men's violence against women.

Perhaps it is helpful to use an analogy, especially one we can all relate to, so indulge me for a moment. It is late 2021 and Australia is fighting its third wave of COVID-19. Community transmission is at an all-time high. It is likely that more households than not have a member who has contracted COVID-19; if you haven't had it yourself, you definitely know someone who has. In fact, the latest statistics suggest that one in four women are now suffering from the virus. In response, politicians are now holding daily briefings, a ministerial taskforce has been established, and every member of the community has a clear role to play, and a responsibility to uphold, in stopping the spread of the virus ...

You'll likely know where I am headed with this. While the above is a hypothetical disaster scenario, the reaction to date to the COVID-19 pandemic has clearly demonstrated that when the political will is there, governments can move quickly and decisively to respond at a national level with the resources and attention that the severity of the issue necessitates. The pandemic has showcased the ability of federal and state/territory governments to work together to identify an issue of common concern and to mobilise across the community to address that threat. Now imagine what it would be like if the range of professionals who can readily recite a COVID-safe action plan all truly understood their roles and responsibilities in keeping women and children safe from domestic, family and sexual violence.

Why have we not seen this degree of national response to violence against women in Australia? Why is it that the same level of funding commitment, coordination and action has not been directed at ensuring the personal safety and wellbeing of half of Australia's population?

I firmly believe that those in power in Australia do not take women's safety seriously—that despite decades of people marching and agitating for change, for many of those who hold power, violence against women continues to be viewed as a private issue.

TACKLING GENDER INEQUALITY

If the aim is to prevent and ultimately eliminate all forms of violence against women in Australia—and let me be clear, that *must* be the aim—then tackling the gender inequality in this country, which I discussed earlier, is pivotal. We simply won't achieve the substantive prevention of men's violence against women without significant progress towards the achievement of gender equality. As former senator Natasha Stott Despoja has said: 'Violence emerges in a broader social construct. This is a society where the underlying conditions of gender inequality mean that violence is often condoned, trivialised or considered a private matter'.[88]

So how does Australia perform against other countries on gender inequality? Every year, the World Economic Forum provides global analyses of the gender gap. In 2006, Australia was ranked fifteenth in the world for gender parity—not exactly a leader on this issue, but perhaps borderline respectable. Fifteen years later, Australia's performance in addressing the gender gap has declined and our position globally is neither leading nor respectable. As of early 2021, Australia ranks fiftieth in the world on the gender gap, which takes into account four measures: economic participation and opportunity, political empowerment, educational attainment, and health and survival.

The Scandinavian nations are well represented as leaders in this space, with Iceland, Finland and Norway taking the top three rankings, followed by our closest neighbour, New Zealand. The United Kingdom sits in twenty-third place, while in the immediate aftermath of Donald Trump's presidency, a four-year term where concerns surrounding the erosion of women's rights were front and centre, the United States appears in thirtieth place, twenty countries above Australia's ranking. Other nations that sit ahead of Australia in their progress towards gender parity are South Africa, Colombia, Albania, Cuba, Serbia and the Philippines, just to name a few.

When you break down Australia's ranking against each of the four aforementioned measures, the results are even more sobering. Our performance on economic participation and opportunity is lower than our overall average—here, Australia sits in seventieth position globally, and on political empowerment we hold the rank of fifty-fourth. But it is our ranking on health and survival that is most telling: on this measure, which takes into account the early death of women due to violence, as well as disease, malnutrition and other factors, we are ninety-ninth in the world.

Interestingly, Australia shares first place with twenty-six other countries for educational attainment; we have some of the most educated women in the world. Yet those same highly educated women experience inequality in so many facets of their lives. They are being killed at a rate of one per week and victimised by men's violence, be it at home, in the workplace or in public.

If we are to make progress on improving women's equality in Australia, we will need to acknowledge where the inequalities exist. These must be named, identified and remedied. We cannot solve a problem that we feel too uncomfortable—or too paralysed by the status quo—to call out. As Kate Jenkins has described, gender inequality is Australia's 'dirty secret'.[89] We know that it is present throughout our workplaces and our parliament, and we know that it is the root cause of violence against women. But we have been so slow in our attempts to address this issue.

In her speech at the 2021 March 4 Justice in Canberra, victim-survivor advocate Saxon Mullins was clear on how to tackle gender inequality. Her call to action targeted the men of Australia:

One in five women have experienced sexual violence. Men, where do you think these perpetrators are hiding? They are your friends. They are your co-workers. They are your football mates, and they are your friends from school. It is not enough to say, 'I would never rape someone.' You would need to think about your behaviours. Do you look the other way when your mate yells at his girlfriend on a night out? Do you complain that people are too sensitive when someone calls out 'you're racist' or 'you're transphobic' remarks? If any of this rings a bell, I remind you, you do not need to imagine that you know someone who perpetrates such an act. Because you don't just know them, you helped them, you helped to create a toxic culture of misogyny, a culture of misogyny and transphobia and racism that has allowed them to thrive.[90]

Saxon is right. While there is undoubtedly much work to be done at the political and community levels, real change cannot occur without a shift in individual responsibility. All Australians have a role to play here. And men must be part of the solution because, ultimately, they are at the heart of the problem.

TRANSFORMATIVE LEADERSHIP

In 2016, Rosie Batty said: 'It's about continuing to point the finger at government, who are way behind the corporate workplace, and saying, "You've got to step up too, you can't have double standards".'[91] Consider the finger pointed. We cannot address our national crisis of violence against women without better leadership from government at all levels—this includes local government and state and territory government, but more importantly the federal government. Violence against women is not simply a women's issue, a private issue, a bespoke problem that only impacts a certain group. It is a whole-of-community problem that requires whole-of-community responses driven by national leadership. Transformative leadership requires a sharp shift in how we understand and respond to men's violence.

As I was in the final stages of writing this book, a federal Cabinet reshuffle was announced. We now have more ministers with portfolio responsibilities for issues relating to women, and specifically women's safety, than ever before. The effectiveness of those portfolios in pushing for real change and driving that at the highest level of the Australian Parliament will only become clear over time, and it would be unfair at this early stage to comment on whether those in the positions allocated have the ability to achieve this. I have to hope they do, otherwise I am resigning myself to the idea that this is still not the moment of change. And it desperately needs to be. I do not want Australian women to be compelled by similar events to march again in a year, five years, or a decade's time.

It has already been four years since women across the United States marched in what was the largest single-day demonstration in US history. While the exact numbers are hard to know, it is estimated that in January 2017, around four million people took to streets across the country as part of the Women's March. The next-largest marches occurred in 1969 and 1970, when up to one million Americans participated in the Vietnam War Moratorium, and in February 2003, when a million Americans demonstrated against the US invasion of Iraq.[92]

I make these comparisons to show that violence against women is no longer a side issue, something that occurs only behind some closed doors and only in some toxic relationships. The millions of women who have marched against gender inequality and men's violence demonstrate this. The issue has been thrust literally out onto the streets.

Transformative leadership requires the creation of genuine partnerships with the community, experts in the field, and importantly, victim-survivors. That engagement must lead to meaningful ways of bringing diverse views to the table and privileging them in decision-making. I am extremely conscious of the fact that this book speaks largely about white women's experiences of male intimate partner violence. While there are nods to diverse experiences where possible, I do not purport to talk about, or for, communities to which I do not belong or with whom I have not consulted. Their voices are far more powerful than mine on this issue, and in acknowledging the short-comings of my own intervention, I implore those with the platforms and leadership to do so to find ways to elevate diverse women's views and experiences.

It is a time to be bold. Too many Australians have come to accept violence against women in a multitude of settings as part and parcel of everyday life, and this absolutely needs to change. The elimination of all forms of violence against women must be the end goal. I refuse to give up on the potential for this change—we must continue to fight for it, because the flip side is just too grim.

We must acknowledge that *The National Plan to Reduce Violence against Women and Their Children 2010–2022* has not lived up to the hopes that surrounded it at the times of its implementation.[93] Introduced by prime minister Julia Gillard in 2009, the plan's objective was to coordinate and amplify the efforts of Australian federal, state and territory governments to achieve a sustained reduction in the levels of violence against women. And yet here we sit ten years later with the same, if not worse, prevalence rates. As the federal government goes about preparing the next national plan, we must reflect honestly on the lack of progress and openly discuss the barriers that continue to impede change. We must learn from the last decade, but at the same time demand more for the next one.

In 2015, when the Victorian Government announced it was directing $36 million towards the establishment of the first Royal Commission into Family Violence, it began to address known failings in the statewide family violence system—failings that contributed to the killings of Luke Batty, Kelly Thompson and many others. In the years since the royal commission reported its findings,[94] the Victorian Government has committed itself to implementing all 227 recommendations, and it has dedicated substantive funding to accomplish this.[95] Approximately $4 billion in funding was committed to delivering the royal commission's road map for reform in the first five years. That $4 billion is more than the total funding committed to family violence across all Australian states and territories and federally. Frighteningly, the Victorian services responding to family violence victim-survivors and people who use violence still turn women away because they do not have the resources to support them. At the same time, men's behaviour-change programs report long waiting lists and unanswered calls due to the underfunding of the services needed to hold perpetrators to account and to keep them in view.[96] This is a wicked problem.

Funding in and of itself will not be enough, but it is an important piece of the puzzle.

The current generation of leaders can push Australia forward in these efforts. They can provide consistent national leadership on this issue, adequately fund whole-of-community responses and prevention efforts, and work with those who share the goal of eliminating men's violence. The Australian Government can address violence against women, our national shame, if its members have the courage and the will to do so.

ACKNOWLEDGEMENTS

It is not every day that I receive a phone call with a proposal to write a book—thank you Louise Adler for giving me the platform to write this book, and for encouraging me to find my own voice within it. And thank you to Paul Smitz for crafting my manuscript to ensure my message is heard, and for doing so in an incredibly supportive way.

This book could not have been written without the research support of Emma McNicol and the master language skills of Tom Beecher. Thank you both for bringing your meticulous attention to detail to this project.

I am so fortunate to work alongside a team of intellectually inspiring dear colleagues at the

Monash Gender and Family Violence Prevention Centre. Particular thanks go to Sandra Walklate, Sharon Pickering, Silke Meyer, Marie Segrave, Jasmine McGowan, Naomi Pfitzner, JaneMaree Maher, Jude McCulloch and Jacqui True. My work is always enhanced by the conversations I have with each of you.

My thanks, as always, go to my husband Michael. Without your support and encouragement, this quite simply would not have been possible. Thank you.

NOTES

1   Tom Stayner, 'How Australian Politics Has Been Shaken to the Core in the Wake of Brittany Higgins' Rape Allegation', SBS News, 2 March 2021.

2   Yan Zhuang, '"Enough is Enough": Thousands across Australia March against Sexual Violence', *The New York Times*, 15 March 2021.

3   SBS News, 'Scott Morrison Speaks on March 4 Justice Rallies, Says Protests Elsewhere Are "Met with Bullets"', 27 March 2021.

4   Ian Gray, 'Finding: Inquest into the Death of Luke Geoffrey Batty', Coroners Court of Victoria, 2015.

5   Thea Brown, Samantha Lyneham, Willow Bryant, Samantha Bricknell, Adam Tomison, Danielle Tyson and Paula Fernandz Arias, *Filicide in Australia, 2000–2012: A National Study*, Australian Institute of Criminology, 2019.

6   Martin McKenzie-Murray, 'Rosie Batty: The Private Toll of Public Grief', *The Saturday Paper*, no. 258, 22–28 June 2019.

7   Marcia Neave, Patricia Faulkner and Tony Nicholson, *Royal Commission into Family Violence: Report and Recommendations*, Victorian Government, March 2016.

8   Georgie Dent, 'Five Women Were Murdered in Australia in Seven Days', *Women's Agenda*, 30 September 2019.

9   Jane Gilmore, 'Six Women Killed in Five Days: You Need to Engage with This Crisis', *The Sydney Morning Herald*, 9 October 2018.

10   Amy Remeikis, 'Linda Reynolds Pays Compensation after Calling Alleged Rape Victim Brittany Higgins "a Lying Cow"', *The Guardian*, 12 March 2021.

11   Rebecca Opie and Olivia Mason, 'Sacked FiveAA Host Jeremy Cordeaux Unapologetic for "Silly Little Girl" Comments, Brittany Higgins Responds', ABC News, 29 March 2021.

12   SBS News, 'Scott Morrison Criticised for Invoking his Daughters in Response to Brittany Higgins' Rape Allegations', 16 February 2021.

13   News.com.au, 'Grace Tame's Australian Press Club Speech in Full', 3 March 2021, https://www.news.com.au/national/politics/grace-tames-australian-press-club-speech-in-full/news-story/2f641d00 3254955a25d754a6a59b1926 (viewed April 2021).

14   Tom Stayner, 'Grace Tame Tells Scott Morrison "Having Children Doesn't Guarantee a Conscience"', SBS News, 3 March 2021.

15   *R v Ramage* [2004] VSC 508, per Osborn J at 22.

16   Ibid. at 33.

17   Ibid. at 63.

18   Ibid. at 10.

19   Ibid. at 46.

20   Karen Kissane, *Silent Death: The Killing of Julie Ramage*, Hodder, Sydney, 2004, p. 184.

21   Ibid.

22   Australian Institute of Health and Welfare, *Family, Domestic and Sexual Violence in Australia*, Canberra, 2018, p. 21; and Domestic and Family Violence Death Review and Advisory Board (Qld), *2018–19 Annual Report*, Queensland Government, 2019.

23   On this, see Kate Fitz-Gibbon, *Homicide Law Reform, Gender and the Provocation Defence: A Comparative Perspective*, Palgrave MacMillan, Hampshire, 2014.

24   Australian Institute of Criminology, *Homicide in Australia 2017–18*, Canberra, 2020.

25   Australian Bureau of Statistics, *Personal Safety, Australia, 2016*, ABS cat. no. 4906.0, 2017.

26   Ibid.

27   Clare Blumer, 'Australian Police Deal with Domestic Violence Every Two Minutes', ABC News, 21 April 2016.

28 Australian Bureau of Statistics, *Personal Safety, Australia, 2016*, ABS cat. no. 4906.0, 2017.

29 Ibid.

30 Australian Bureau of Statistics, *National Aboriginal and Torres Strait Islander Social Survey, 2014–2015*, ABS cat. no. 4729.9. Canberra, 2019.

31 Sue-Anne Hunter, 'Aboriginal Women Have Fought against Gendered Violence Perpetrated by White Men Since Day One', *Women's Agenda*, March 2021.

32 Human Rights Law Centre and Change the Record, *Over-Represented and Overlooked: The Crisis of Aboriginal and Torres Strait Islander Women's Growing Over-Imprisonment*, Victoria and New South Wales, 2017.

33 Bronwyn Carlson, 'No Public Outrage, No Vigils: Australia's Silence at Violence against Indigenous Women', *The Conversation*, 16 April 2021.

34 World Health Organization, *Understanding and Addressing Violence against Women*, Geneva, 2012.

35 Australian Human Rights Commission, *Respect@Work: National Inquiry into Sexual Harassment in Australian Workplaces*, Canberra, 2020.

36 Michaela Whitbourn, 'How One Case Helped Shape Workplace Sexual Harassment Lawsuits', *The Sydney Morning Herald*, 29 March 2021.

37 Australian Human Rights Commission, *Respect@Work: National Inquiry into Sexual Harassment in Australian Workplaces*, Canberra, 2020.

38 J Mouzos and M Segrave, *Homicide in Australia: 2002–2003 National Homicide Monitoring Program (NHMP) Annual Report*, Research and Public Policy Series, no. 55, 2004.

39 Chloe Brice, 'Jill Meagher: Conviction Documentary Reveals How Killer Adrian Bayley Was Caught', ABC News, 3 February 2017.

40 Sarah Krasnostein, 'A Man Who Hates Women', *The Monthly*, October 2019.

41 Melissa Davey, 'Masa Vukotic Had the Right to Be in a Park Alone: Victoria Police Must Apologise for Saying She Didn't', *The Guardian*, 20 March 2015.

42 As quoted in Jo Lauder, 'Victorian Premier Reacts to Eurydice Dixon's Killing', ABC Triple J Hack, 15 June 2018.

43 Domestic Violence Service Australia, *A History of Reclaim the Night*, 4 October 2018.

44 Tom Meagher, 'The Danger of the Monster Myth', ABC News, 18 April 2014.

45 Australian Bureau of Statistics, *Personal Safety, Australia, 2016*, ABS cat. no. 4906.0, 2017.

46 Marcia Neave, Patricia Faulkner and Tony Nicholson, *Royal Commission into Family Violence: Report and Recommendations*, Victorian Government, March 2016, p. 36.

47 Brain Injury Australia, *The Prevalence of Acquired Brain Injury among Victims and Perpetrators of Family Violence*, Sydney, 2018.

48 N Heath, 'A Tragic Reality: Domestic Violence Is the Main Cause of Homelessness for Women', SBS Voices, 10 June 2017.

49 Australian Institute of Health and Welfare, *Australia's Welfare 2017*, no. 13, AUS 214, Canberra, 2017.

50 E Stark, *Coercive Control: The Entrapment of Women in Personal Life*, Oxford University Press, USA, 2009.

51 NSW Government, *Coercive Control: Discussion Paper*, Sydney, October 2020.

52 Ibid.

53 NSW Domestic Violence Death Review Team, *Domestic Violence Death Review Team Report 2015–2017*, Sydney, 2020.

54 Hayley Gleeson, 'Hannah Clarke "Did Everything" She Could to Protect Herself and Her Children. Experts Explain Why It Wasn't Enough', ABC News, 10 March 2020.

55 As cited in Rachel Riga, 'Hannah Clarke's Parents Push for Coercive Control to Be Made a Crime One Year on from Horrific Murders', ABC News, 14 February 2021.

56 Madonna King, '"Intimate Terrorism": Why the Murders of Hannah, Aaliyah, Laianah and Trey Must Spark Change', *The Sydney Morning Herald*, 20 November 2020.

57 *United Nations Women News*, 'The Economic Costs of Violence against Women', 21 September 2016.

58 Australian Government, *Women's Economic Security Statement 2020*, Canberra, 2020, p. 62.

59 Ibid.

60 Deloitte, *The Economic Costs of Sexual Harassment in the Workplace: Final Report*, Canberra, 2019.

61 Australian Government, *Women's Economic Security Statement 2020*, Canberra, 2020, p. 63.

62 Georgie Dent, 'That Women Are the Losers in *This* History-Making Big-Spending Budget Is Shameful', *Women's Agenda*, 6 October 2020.

63 *United Nation Women News*, 'COVID-19 and Its Economic Toll on Women: The Story behind the Numbers', 16 September 2020.

64 D Wood, K Griffiths and T Cowley, *Women's Work: The Impact of the COVID Crisis on Australian Women*, Grattan Institute, 7 March 2021.

65 K Fitz-Gibbon, J McCulloch and J Maher, 'Little in Budget to Counter Family Violence', *The Age*, 4 May 2016.

66 Commonwealth of Australia, 'Budget 2016–17 Overview', 3 May 2016.

67 K Fitz-Gibbon, J McCulloch and J Maher, 'Little in Budget to Counter Family Violence', *The Age*, 4 May 2016.

68 Deborah Anderson and Daniel Saunders, 'Leaving an Abusive Partner: An Empirical Review of Predictors, the Process of Leaving, and Psychological Well-Being', *Trauma, Violence & Abuse*, vol. 4, no. 2, p. 171.

69 *United Nation Women News*, 'Violence against Women and Girls: The Shadow Pandemic—Statement By Phumzile Mlambo-Ngcuka', 6 April 2020.

70 Haley Ott, '6 Months of Coronavirus Lockdown Could Mean 31 Million More Cases of Domestic Violence, UN Says', CBS News, 28 April 2020.

71 United Nations, *Global Study on Homicide: Gender-Related Killing of Women and Girls*, United Nations Office on Drugs and Crime, Vienna, 2018.

72 N Pfitzner, K Fitz-Gibbon and J True, *Responding to the Shadow Pandemic: Practitioner Views on the Nature of and Responses to Violence against Women in Victoria, Australia during the COVID-19 Restrictions*, Monash Gender and Family Violence Prevention Centre, Monash University, Victoria, 2020.

73　E Graham-Harrison, A Giuffrida, H Smith and L Ford, 'Lockdowns around the World Bring Rise in Domestic Violence', *The Guardian*, 28 March 2020.

74　Judith Ireland, 'Malcolm Turnbull's Scathing Attack on Men Who Commit Domestic Violence', *The Sydney Morning Herald*, 24 September 2015.

75　Australian Government Workplace Gender Equality Agency, 'Gender Workplace Statistics at a Glance', 25 February 2021.

76　*The Sydney Morning Herald*, 'Transcript of Julia Gillard's Speech', 10 October 2012.

77　Virginia Haussegger, 'The Politics of Women's Political Representation: Anne Summers' National Press Club Address', *Broad Agenda*, 6 March 2019.

78　See EG Ferris, *Refugee Women and Violence*, World Council of Churches, Geneva, 1990; and C Cockburn, 'The Continuum of Violence: A Gender Perspective on Violence and Peace', in W Giles and J Hyndmann (eds), *Sites of Violence: Gender and Conflict Zones*, University of California Press, Berkeley, 2004.

79　*R v Freeman* [2011] VSC 139, per Coghlan J at 55.

80　M Perkins, 'Thompson, Stabbed to Death by Ex-Partner: Coroner', *The Age*, 21 April 2016.

81　Coroners Court of Victoria, *Inquest into the Death of Kelly Ann Thompson*, file no. COR 2014 000824.

82　Ibid.

83　Tarang Chawla, '"No One Said Anything": The Familiar Narrative of Kim Murphy's Needless Death', Our Watch, 27 April 2020.

84　Bension Siebert, 'Man Charged with Murder after Woman's Body Found at Morphett Vale House', ABC News, 17 April 2020.

85　Australian Bureau of Statistics, *Personal Safety, Australia, 2016*, ABS cat. no. 4906.0, 2017.

86　Rosie Batty, 'Rosie Batty's Outgoing Australian of the Year Speech', Our Watch, 27 January 2016.

87　News.com.au, 'Grace Tame's Australian Press Club Speech in Full', 3 March 2021, https://www.news.com.au/national/politics/grace-tames-australian-press-club-speech-in-full/news-story/2f641d00 3254955a25d754a6a59b1926 (viewed April 2021).

88 Natasha Stott Despoja, 'Natasha Stott Despoja, Chair of Our Watch, Addresses the National Press Club, 19 August 2020', Our Watch, 20 August 2020.

89 Kate Jenkins, 'Accelerating Change: Gender Equality from the Household to the Workplace', address, National Press Club, 20 April 2016.

90 R Dexter, '"Men, Where Do You Think These Perpetrators Are Hiding?" Saxon Mullins Calls for Change', The Sydney Morning Herald, 15 March 2021.

91 Xavier Smerdon, 'Income Inequality Key to Domestic Violence: Rosie Batty', Pro Bono Australia, March 2016.

92 Erica Chenoweth and Jeremy Pressman, 'This Is What We Learned By Counting the Women's Marches', The Washington Post, 7 February 2017.

93 Department of Social Services, Australian Government, The National Plan to Reduce Violence against Women and their Children 2010–2022, Canberra, February 2011.

94 Marcia Neave, Patricia Faulkner and Tony Nicholson, Royal Commission into Family Violence: Report and Recommendations, Victorian Government, March 2016.

95 Department of Premier and Cabinet, Victorian Government, Ending Family Violence: Victoria's Plan for Change, Melbourne, 2016.

96 Tammy Mills, '"Urgent Need": Violent Men Facing Delays in Getting Help Amid Pandemic', The Age, 16 July 2020.

IN THE NATIONAL INTEREST

Other books on the issues that matter: